The Spiritual Magic of a Queer POC:

Inspiration and Practices to Empower the

People of Color

and

Queer Communities to Live in Their

Spiritual Truth

By Shaunna Williams

The Magic Behind It

This is an introductory book of more to come, but I had to get these pages, words, and truths to you now. I needed to speak directly to my queer and people of color communities to remove the veil of separation from spirit and spiritual magic placed on us by history, society, and white male interpreted bible scriptures.

We are in an age where there is no more time to hide from the magic we each possess. It is time that we let go of fear, limiting beliefs, cultural norms, and the harms done to us so we may move forward with the fire ignited within our souls. It is time for us to remember who we are, why we are here, and what we are capable of.

I could not go another moment without using my story, up to this point, to shake you awake from the many sleeps you fall into.

It is my honor to share in this journey with you. It was my destiny to have these experiences to support in our awakening.

My hope is that this book, my story, and my light sparks the fire within you. May you allow each word, page, and moment to open your heart so you may realize something that's divinely amazing about you.

Chapter 1

Jesus is NOT My Religion

OK, bear with me, I know, I know, I came out hot but there was no better way than to introduce you to the fire I carry. I am the middle child, only girl, and an Aries. Stereotype me if you wish...

I was born to two military parents but around the time I made my debut they were just getting adjusted to civilian life. My brothers and I somehow grew up in the church. No matter where in the world we had landed, we always found ourselves a church pew to occupy. Do not let it fool you to think we had a normal church going life because as often as we went to church is as often as life was falling apart around us.

My dad was an abusive addict whose rage targeted my mother and brothers. That's not to say that I never met his wrath but at this point in the story, he was only after my older brother. One night my mom was doing her best to protect my brother when my dad put a gun to her head and threatened her life. That would be the first night she tried to plan our escape from my dad.

Eventually, my mom and older brother were able to fight their way out from under my dad's fist, but my younger brother and I had to endure his fury a bit longer.
Alright, back to Jesus and the church...

Growing up, "he" was painted as this being that was the gatekeeper to heaven, the one we owed everything to because he gave up his life for us.

In all truth, I do think the story of Jesus is beautifully interesting and that he is amongst the highest in the spiritual realm, however, I was never able to believe what I had been

2

taught. I also struggled with the concept that in order to make our way to God we had to go through this being that just died, rose from the dead and then died again. I just kept asking... why do we have to go through Jesus to get to God? Literally, as a kid I would ask whoever I could and was never given any real answer, I was either retold the story of the sacrifice and the holy trinity or told that's just how it is. I also found deep issue and sadness that this Jesus would punish certain people and deem others more holy.

We had certain churches we'd attend depending on where we were. The one I remember most was the church of my grandfather. It was a small church right by his house and we would walk there every Sunday. I was in the choir which I truly enjoyed singing in. Later I was in a gospel group with some other beautiful black ladies. As I got older, other churches began to infiltrate our neighborhood. Looking back, what I always appreciated most about these churches were their willingness to give back to inner city community. Witnessing this introduced to me to servitude.

Having so many churches in my neighborhood allowed me to explore other denominations, attend camps, and see other ways of living. Regardless of this exploration, I found myself being blocked whenever I heard that I needed to go through Jesus or that certain people were chosen while others punished.

Let me tell you though, as much as my soul knew none of these things were true the lies still seeped into my skin. I started to believe in a damning, punishing God. I started to believe certain people were bad and, most frightening, I believed I was disempowered. My disempowerment looked like me believing I had no other options or choices but to suffer in my life, that I was unloved by God, and I had no power or choices to change the trajectory of my life.

When we feel and become disempowered, fear, guilt, shame, and other dense emotions feed the cycle. I believe disempowerment is a tool that men used to build churches and followers. This runs very deeply in the religious society and bleeds over into the reality of many of us. I can tell you that even writing the title for this chapter I felt like my mom was disapproving and could hear my granny saying "God's gonna get you!". I tell you, it's deep, but today I stand in my power and truth and move right along with a smile.

I gave myself permission to free myself from the religion I was raised on when I was about 15 years old and it opened my eyes to vastness of experiences within this world. I was VERY rebellious as a teen and despite the freedom I gave myself and my lack of extreme ties to Christianity, I still would freely attend Christian events out of comfortability and curiosity. I always loved people and different types of people, to be exact... in high school I became pretty "emo" and poetic, but I hung out with all of the different cliques. Remember, when you were in school and all the boxes we created around one another? Yeah, I hung out in all those boxes.

As I mentioned, I would still attend some Christian events, I would attend the morning worship service at school (I grew up in the Bible Belt and services were held in public schools), paying witness to the kids praise but then those same kids would act like complete assholes once the service was over. While I had already experienced this behavior in my own family, the actions of these kids woke me up to another level of hypocrisy. At this point in my life, I just saw hypocrites, not people on their own journey. Regardless, it was simply ammo for my case.

On different occasions in my life I had "weird" experiences with the church and religion. There was a burning bush moment (instantaneous ah ha or revelations of spirit), moments where I absolutely hated God and thought my anger with them would overtake me. Then there were moments where I could feel their presence, undeniable moments where I was protected by higher realms. In hindsight, I can now see how these moments were stepping stones that led me to the spiritual freedom I have found and allowed me to become the teacher I am today. Though it may have been painful and confusing, I am grateful for every moment of the journey.

Now let's talk more on my moments of hatred and anger towards God.

Chapter 2

The Wrath

My experience after some spiritual deep diving and wet breathwork shaped my belief that I did not want to be born into this lifetime nor deal with all that it entails. However, I've learned that I was basically kicked through the birth canal because I was needed here. This resistance before my birth created the context for a constantly pissed off experience as a child, teenager, and even moments as an adult.

I'll tell you the ugly part first, which, I've not admitted publicly so please be easy on me.

After my dad beat me and almost killed my little brother, we were taken away from him and placed in foster care (a traumatic experience I will not discuss at this point), until my granny adopted us. We had gone from one hell to another and then to the hell of my granny's. I had never felt so much hatred before in my life or that my own family was against me. She was an active alcoholic and was taking care of three kids while my mother was across the street addicted to crack. Needless to say, she had her reasons to be angry, but that wasn't my doing. I felt she hated me with every bone in her body. She would say hateful abusive things often telling me that I wasn't anything, I was going to hell, I remind her of my dad and I'm just like him all at the impressionable age of 8. I was so afraid of what my grandmother would do to me that I was scared to eat food that she prepared as I thought she would try to kill me.

We had court appointed social workers and counselors who I'd always plead with to let me go back with my dad or would beg other people to adopt me. At one point I got to speak with my dad and we planned him coming to get me. I would pack my bags and anytime my granny would attack me I would tell her that he was coming to get me. She would laugh and tell me he's never coming.

She was right. Strike 8, God.

I became very angry and disappointed with my life experience before I was 10 years old. I had heard "God's going to get you!" so much that I took this on by authorizing God to get my granny since she was such a bad person. They didn't.

Strike 15, God.

I feel I need to make this side note as I'm very grateful that my God appointed hit on my granny didn't stand. As I got older, we were given the opportunity to repair our relationship and I now know just how deeply she loves me.

By this time, I had experienced several episodes of rape and molestation. One was with a man, who had to be in his late 60s, that would molest little girls and pay them money...I was an 8-year-old prostitute.

At this point, I felt that I was responsible to take care of my little brother and myself. I felt that I was his mother and took on that role. When my mom went to jail for the last time and got clean, she got us back.

Let me tell you, she had two pissed off and wild children at this time. Why were we not enough for her to quit while we were younger before we were teenagers?

Strike 20, God.

By the time I had moved back in with my mom, I was in my own full-blown addiction. I believe during that drugs helped me to survive. I had no other tools that made me feel like life was worth living. I know I caused my mom so much worry and stress. I was living a double life: searching spiritually and showing up in the church but dying inside from my own addiction. At one point, around 16, I wanted to die. I couldn't take this life anymore. I took a bunch of pills in hopes of committing suicide and leaving this existence. I didn't die.

Strike 50, God.

Somewhere along the way I got into going to shows, being in bands, and living this teenage girl rocker lifestyle. I was the bass player for a band called Jailbait Pinups. Music (and food) became my escape and my first lifesaver.

One spring my friends and I went to a Guster and Phantom Planet show where I met Arthur. Arthur was in college and I was underage. We connected in a platonic, respectful, safe, and intimate way. My friends had abandoned me, so he and I sat and talked. It was during this conversation that he introduced me to Wicca. Gasp! Right, the Devil's religion! He was the nicest person that I had ever met up to this point. He taught me a few things and recommended I get the book, *Goddess Initiation* by Francesca De Grandis.

Picture this: teenage me in the back of my yard, in the projects, casting spells and doing magic. I'm sitting in a circle in the hood! I can bet you I was the ONLY one. Around this time, I started having dark dreams. I felt like I was suffocating, that darkness was covering me. These dreams were debilitating and I couldn't move. THIS freaked me the fuck out. I threw away the book and promptly stopped studying Wicca.

At the time, I didn't know my dreams were probably because of my dark acts: using drugs, wanting to die, and not being clear or guided with what I was inviting in. Dark and light cannot coexist within the same velocity for long within the same person. At some point we choose which side of the fence we want to be on. I chose to continue using drugs and stop doing magic. I mark this moment in my life as supporting future moments in my life.

When I turned 17 and was kicked out of my mom's. We had a "tiny" altercation where I threatened lives with a knife. I was homeless for the first time. When my granny wouldn't take me in a friend's mom let me stay with her, as long as I stopped using and got help. This lady was an angel of mine and I am forever grateful. I couldn't stop stealing her pills but the day after I graduated high school, May 16, 2004, I went into treatment.

While I was there, I was angry and blamed my mother for everything, but she gave me a key piece of information that changed my life instantly. "Shaunna, I was not able to be the parent you needed as a child and for that I am sorry but your life now and at this point is all your doing. You can't blame me for this- you are responsible." Woah! But but but I'm so angry!!!

I was now prepared to shift my lenses a little bit. I was now ready to drop some of my anger and blame towards my mother, but it all went inward and ignited my self-hatred. This dramatic shift to extreme self-loathing exacerbated my eating disorder. Yes, I developed an eating disorder along the way. I was a binge eater and bulimic, which started around freshman year of high school.

11

We are not going to put too much focus on this here, though I will say there's a preconceived notion that eating disorders are limited to white women and it isn't true. It doesn't discriminate- no self-sabotaging behaviors ever do.

Now that I had adjusted my lenses, exposed some secrets in treatment, almost got kicked out, and had some God experiences, I was ready to see what was ahead of me. I had now discovered a beginner's level of shift finding a hopefulness I had never before experienced.

Chapter 3

Burning Bush

Experience

In the Big Book of Alcoholics Anonymous it talks about spiritual experiences, noting that some can be "burning bush" experiences or some can be of the educational variety. I've experienced both since 2004 that I've been consciously aware of.

I was fresh out of treatment, which provided a few great moments of revealing the realness of God- situations that are unexplainable. As I mentioned, my eating disorder was in high gear. While working in a small pharmacy I met a friend from high school. We got to talking and discovered that we shared the same eating disorder. We instantly formed a bond in sickness. She taught me tricks of the illness and we could share with one another things neither of us had been able to share before. Through this, I became very sick. If I wasn't throwing up, I was running or doing both.

One night I was running away from myself and burning off the food. I was running the same route as I always did. By the time I got to the end of the road I heard loud and clear: "You stopped so you didn't kill yourself with drugs and alcohol, but this will kill you just the same." I stopped dead where I was and started crying, I was balling, actually. I fell completely to my knees not knowing how to get through this.

I decided to start talking about it with people that didn't have this same illness or that were in recovery from this illness. When I reached 90 days of sobriety, I was able to move into a halfway house with great structure and programming. Both would prove to be beneficial to my recovery.

Here, I was introduced to guided meditation which opened me up to studying Buddhism. I was also introduced to the fitness industry and I began my journey with both.

Buddhism and meditation brought about a freedom I didn't know I was looking for. It allowed me to be with me and introduced new concepts such as compassion, forgiveness, non-attachment, kindness, and presence. These concepts were foreign to me up to this point. I started attending any sits, retreats, or day-longs that were offered.

I had freedom from believing a certain way, freedom from all the questions I had with Christianity, and the freedom to go inward. Up to this point everything was outside of me, I only knew how to seek Spirit outwardly.

Chapter 4

The.

Fucking.

Backslide.

I am writing a complete book on this chapter and that is the weight that it carries. So, stay tuned.

I was moving right along in life in a forward momentum. I was sober, had "healthy" friends, my own place, and was progressing spiritually. I must say that sitting here gearing up to write this chapter pisses me off. I hate that this is a chapter in my life. I hate that this period in my life carries such weight that a book has to be written about it. It still hurts, even with being able to see the good, the light, and the great possibilities of creating a movement and non-profit to empower others spiritually. It hurts to even think the words "I'm grateful for this." It is an area God and I don't see eye-to-eye on. We do not have to and I am OK with that today.

On April 26, 2005, I had just turned 19 and my little brother was 17. On this day the Feds busted down my grandmother's door, destroyed her house, and arrested my brother. Earlier in the day, the news had another suspect that the police were looking for. He had the gun, disposed of it, changed his clothes, and fled the city. All while my little brother was just chilling at my granny's like normal.

When we found out that my brother was being charged with first degree murder we all rushed down to the juvenile detention center to be with him. We had no means for a lawyer, no wherewithal, and we were living our worst nightmare.

Jamiel has always claimed his innocence. Given his stance, the lack of sufficient "evidence," and shaky witnesses accounts, we believed the truth would prevail. My family decided to put our efforts in prayer circles while gaining support from the church and friends to get Jamiel a good lawyer. We knew that we had God on our side and that Jamiel would be free.

The trial lasted about six months until finally reaching a verdict. Throughout the trial I saw childhood friends turn against my brother or because of the old street code refuse to speak up for him. There was one witness that told the absolute truth giving evidence of doubt. Eventually even our own family turned against us pushing to get plea deals from the state. As we continued to push for appeals and retrials, the truth of their lies began to come out. It was too little too late as he had already been sentenced to life in prison and Williamson County Judicial System were set in their ways. We put our faith in his lawyer and God. The same lawyer who told him not to take the stand. The state offered a plea of 15 years, but we turned it down. We believed the truth would prevail. My oldest brother played private investigator for the lawyer.

He was only 21 at the time, though some post-conviction documents state he was 26. I guess the lawyer was trying to prove he was older and more aware. In the end, the lawyer and God let us down.

I witnessed the light and faith within my brothers, my mom, and myself begin to dim and shut off. In an instant we were no longer the same people. There is no way to prepare for a situation like this. There is no rule book and no way to know. When faith is tested, and God seems to have dropped you, it creates the way for an ugly path.

I had never felt this level of hatred towards people, God, and faith before in my life. It all had been wearing on me since the night he was arrested. I was feeling emotions I had never felt sober. I did not understand them, and the anger was taking over. I would talk to my sponsor at the time about how I wanted to use and how I kept praying but my desire was still there. I planned to drink and found some friends that would support me in that plan. I believed I could use and still stay spiritually connected, but as soon as I drank, everything went dark. It was an instant disconnect and yet another lesson that light and dark can't coexist. I found myself sick, without a car, hitchhiking, and making promises to never use again. I continued using for close to two years and my life was sad, depressing, and frightening.

Chapter 5

Emerging from the

Dark

During those two years, I figured it was a fine time in my life to come out.

You know, as a lover of women. I had attended Pride festivals as a teenager and put the equality stickers on my mom's car. Low and behold, I came-out to my mother as we were walking at Centennial Park and the Pride festival was setting up- OH, the irony!

My first girlfriend was when I was in 5th grade, her name was Charlene. Obviously, in the South it wasn't accepted. She was banished from coming over and I was told we would go to hell. That kept me pretty "straight" for some time.

Back to coming out- I'm at this park doing laps with my mother and she is baffled. She is stunned as it caught her completely by surprise. She asked what happened to me to make me this way and I told her that nothing happened, it is just who I am. She proceeded to love me as she always had and didn't condemn me or anything, but she also didn't want people to know. My little brother told me I was going to hell and my older brother didn't understand it. Today, they all support me fully. I love people, I'm fluid-queer and would prefer no labels unless they are dividing the straights and the gays, or we are rallying.

I met my official first girlfriend when I was 19 (cue Tegan and Sarah's "Nineteen"). I was smitten! She was a few years older than me, a drummer in a band, Italian, and gorgeous. She was the calmest person I had ever met. I truly believe she was a God-send to me in this time, she helped keep me alive. Life was in the fast lane; I was working in fitness and bars, and many crazy events happened. I cheated, she cheated, it was a cycle. She fed me life and love while another woman fed me alcohol and pills. It lasted until I got sober again at 21 years old.

I was working at a bar and music lounge in East Nashville when I began to feel the energy of other people. This made me start to realize I was a little different. When the panic attacks started, God presented two teachers for me who took me under their wings teaching me about Reiki and how to protect my energy. Prior to meeting my teachers, I had no clue what Reiki was, and one key teaching was that I didn't have to believe or know. They gave me a book to assist in my studying.

One day, I was at a party with alcohol flowing and surrounded by friends. I felt alone and like I was having an out of body experience and I had the realization that I can't live like these people, I had to stop drinking and I had to stop pretending.

When I woke up the next day I promised to go to a meeting, but found myself sitting at a crystal shop crying, not wanting to go in when a random guy asked me what was wrong.

I told him I was scared to go, and he said to me "it's not going to hurt you to go- nothing bad will happen." That day is my sobriety date, May 21, 2007. I came in angry because I thought I could drink and maintain my spiritual condition as well as not deal with what was happening with my brother. I was wrong and no stubborn Aries likes being wrong.

I started working at a resort hotel in town and I had so much anxiety working there. I would pray "God please remove my anxiety and direct me towards what you have me to be." One day in walked my next spiritual teacher, Ataana, and his wife. He supported me greatly in my evolution and helped me deal with my emotions around what happened with my brother. We worked on my anger and he taught me this mantra that I could use for anything: "I no longer choose the vibration required to manifest the energy of anger in my life." He had me say these 100 times a day for 40 days. I did it! I was willing to be free from these body snatchers; anger, rage, sadness, survivor's guilt. I felt I was finally emerging from this darkness.

Chapter 6

Capacity for Harm Done

I've done all the extreme religious practices and trying to prove my worth and existence through someone else's rules and misguidance. My hope is that this book allows you to stop trying to fight for, or prove, you're worthy to exist.

The first time I remember feeling that I was less than and unworthy was during my teenage years. This was after all the stuff of my childhood and reiterated by someone outside of my family. I thought I had made friends, they were white, and we got into a ton of nonsense together. I was normally the only black person with an occasional additional black person in the mix.

I was at my "friend" Luke's house and I had made a remark on how nice his mother was, and he said to me: "She's only nice to you because she feels sorry for you." I was stunned. I felt like I was punched in the gut. I asked "Why?" and he said, "It's because you are black and live in the projects." In that moment I learned the limiting beliefs that "I'm not good enough" and "I'm not an equal person to white people". It also made me feel distant from the people I was friends with. I heard often "you're the whitest black person we know" and "...but we like you though". As if I was the chosen black girl to be amongst the white people.

This is not about racism though these fuckers were racist, the bigger picture is how powerful words can be, how we harm people with our prejudice and how great of an impact ignorance can create. I always felt like I was a charity case for white people or people of the church. Not all my encounters and people were like this though I had an amazing friend, Catherine. I basically lived at her house and her family was loving. They welcomed me in even though Cat and I got into lots of trouble.

Spiritual shame is quite possibly the worst form of shame. You have a whole church, additional churches, and the word of the Bible reaffirming it for you. As I've mentioned, I've had "weird moments" in the church. One moment in particular, I was attending this mega-church. It was hip, it was cool, and the worship portion was a live concert. I had been assigned a mentor and her sole purpose was to lead me to Jesus and make me a member of this church. This was a non-denominational church that still believed that either you speak in tongues or you interpret the language. I found myself in this area of the church that seemed secretive and in this military type of experience that was supposed to give me the ability to speak in or interpret tongues.

I'm not sure how much time was put into this because I disassociated, but I was not able to speak in tongues or understand them. When they came to me and I told them my results, they responded: "something is blocking you from God." But what I heard was "something is wrong with you and you are not worthy".

I've done weird fasts to get closer to God. I've done celibacy oaths with the intention of getting closer to God. I've ventured into Pentecostal, Seventh Day Adventist, Catholic churches, and synagogues. All of these experiences played some role in my path. The church that supported my path and had a universal mindset was Unity of Nashville. This church let me know that all I was feeling and thinking was true. There, I learned that God is in us all and the biggest thing was love. Unity really spoke into the love of God not discriminating. I found this church because a friend of mine attended their "A Course in Miracles" group. This was the first church that I became involved in from the alignment in my heart. I was a Sunday school teacher, I'd attend events, I'd bring my girlfriends, and would feel comfortable holding their hand. I am forever grateful for this church.

Along the way I battled with the traditional church's view on the gays and homosexuality as sin. I believed this most of my life and it kept me closeted. Even after I came out there was a sense of shame or judgement. My mom told me that she loved and accepted me, but I was still sinning. I mean who isn't, really?

People that are Christians that use the Bible and word of God to support their hate, confusion, and ignorance are not worthy to keep us from our spiritual truth. These people are misguided, scared, and living in an old paradigm. A lower form of our human experience is for us to feel superior to others and to hold others under thumb. These actions have historically served no one.

It is our individual responsibility to access forgiveness and give ourselves spiritual freedom. Today I have no animosity towards the church because I know the truth. I can walk into any church or congregation and not feel anger or uncomfortability. We all deserve this level of freedom and choice. Whether you wish to be involved in the church, start a new spiritual practice, do silent spiritual retreats, magic, energy healing and/or inward truth practices, it all starts with self-permission and forgiveness.

We have some unlearning to do but above that we have reclaiming to do. Say it with me: I am worthy of any space I occupy!

God loves me! I am a divine being and I hold magic in me! Now pick up your head and go forth in power!

Chapter 7

From the Ashes I Have Risen

I had been so conditioned to thrive in "tough" situations or "shit hitting the fan" moments that I had no clue what to do in calm moments where I or someone else wasn't wreaking havoc on my life. I had operated from the default of fight or flight and I needed to learn how to be still, in my body and build trust within myself and Spirit.

I have invested my life to expand my capacity of being still, in my body and deepening my trust of self and Spirit. It was hard for me to put full trust in anything outside of myself and ironically, I did not have much trust in myself. It takes commitment, work, love, compassion, and a willingness to keep digging, growing, and living. It's OK if you don't feel like you possess all of these now, focus on what you do possess and keep moving forward.

This book has revealed only a quarter of my life's story, but I wanted to provide you all with enough to know who I am a little, where I've come from, and some of who I am today.

I am an ordained Minister with a Universal approach, Reiki Master, Breathwork Practitioner, Spiritual Teacher and Coach, Body Freedom Coach, Humanitarian, Expression Empowerment Leader, human etc. I leave space for my continuous expansion, remembering and learning of my divine gifts.

I facilitate workshops and speak, I teach movement and connection as well as help others find healing and divine truth within.

I hold substance-free spiritual ceremonies for groups and ordain weddings. I am proud of my evolution and my lioness gumption to keep going.

I aim to live free from the lies that pain has to come before growth, that suffering is a part of life that there is only a certain amount of good in life that I can experience as well as all the ancestral and subconscious unlearning. In place of these things I welcome ease, joy, bliss, grace, expansion, and truth.

Consciously, my spiritual awakening started in 2004 when I first made the decision to stop killing myself with substances and my eating disorder. 12 Step recovery supported me in building a solid foundation for my truth to unfold. I needed to first put down those vices so I could finally see myself. I needed to be of clear mind, soul, spirit, and body. I now fully understand and believe that mood-altering substances creates a disconnect in consciousness. It creates a lower vibration in the body, altering our divine connection- the connection that is innately in us.

I have continued to surrender over and over again, to something higher than my human self: a higher power, God, Spirit, Universe, Hierarchy of Light, ad infinitum. The first time I felt surrender in my bones, I had two elements that have been spiritual vortexes for me, nature and music.

I was in my favorite area within Percy Warner Park and I was listening to "Surrender" by The Barlow Girls. I wept and I felt as if I wasn't alone (I probably then played "Never Alone"). This was the first time I truly felt I could trust that a Higher Power was with me. It was as if my body had admitted exhaustion and my soul was telling me to give up the fight against truth. I can't really put words to it, but I felt it and it was real!

When we truly connect to the truth that we are not alone at which point deep healing can begin. There are things that happen when we tap in to our spirit, and there is a lot of fear around "crazy supernatural" stuff. I believe as long as we stay in the light and are protected by the light, we are taken care of. So, I say allow yourself to be in full discovery (seek and explore) of your spiritual truths and gifts. When you are ready for the next level of knowing and remembering, opportunity will appear. Trust me, this is where our true power lies.

I want you to be able to experience some of the practices that have supported my continuous spiritual transformation.

I want to empower you to try them out in the comfort of your home or invite your family, friends, or colleagues to join you.

All that you'll need is the willingness, open-mindedness, and a tiny bit of belief to keep taking the next step and following through. The last chapters are dedicated solely to practices.

I believe in you- so let's do this!

Chapter 8

Sobriety Practice

Don't put the book down!

Hear me out.

I am not saying that everyone is addicted to substances, but I am saying everyone can benefit from sobriety. If you are drinking or using benzos heavily or daily, you'll want to seek medical supervision. If you are using opiates daily, then you may also want to have medical supervision, but your detox process isn't fatal. If you have a regular habit of substance use, make sure you get support. If you are not sure if your habit is regular and heavy or not you can get a drug and alcohol use disorder assessment from a licensed drug and alcohol abuse counselor. I repeat: DO NOT do this without therapeutic or medical consult if you are a habitual, heavy, or regular user.

This step takes divine honesty with yourself. Take a moment, ask for guidance, and assess your life. A tribe and community built of healthy, honest, and supportive people are essential for sustaining sobriety. There are resources available to you all over the world. There are 12 step groups, religious recovery-based groups: Celebrate Recovery and Refuge Recovery, SMART recovery, and people all over the world discovering the importance of a sober lifestyle. Do not go at this step alone! I am here to support and connect you to any resources you may need.

I advise in this practice to discontinue all self-sabotaging and addictive behavior: cutting, self- harm, sex, shopping, eating disorders, gambling, etc.- anything that blocks you from you, health, and Spirit. There are support groups, books, professionals, and additional resources for you.

This is an invitation for you to take an oath of sobriety. If you are smoking pot daily or less than daily or using other substances infrequently you may not need too much outside assistance. If this becomes hard for you, get help.

You will want support: community and tribe are key.

You want to pick a timeframe that you will not use any mood-or-mind-altering substances, I suggest no less than 30 days. I have experienced people taking sobriety oaths and after it's finished, they deep dive back into using as they were before. This is not advised.

Allow yourself to shift inward during this time of being sober.

Ask yourself the following questions as often as possible:

What am I covering up with my need, desire, obsession or compulsion to use mood- and mind-altering substances?

What do I need to heal and give love to?

What are my beliefs and values?

What is my divine purpose in this life?

Who can support me in moving forward?

When you start to receive insights to yourself, honor them. If you are clear on an action to take, a wound to start healing or to bring deeper healing to, your calling, a certification, or idea you need to build on, start taking immediate action.

In this time of sobriety your head will become much clearer, but first, it must move through the chatter that's been holding you back. Brave through this process with support and know that the rewards far outweigh the temporary discomfort and pain. I can tell you that on the other side it was all worth it!

Allow yourself to start to try new things. If there is a class you have been wanting to attend, do so. A group you've been wanting to check out? Go! Anything that will move you forward and decrease any fear that's been holding you back, I urge you to do!

When I first got sober, I didn't know what to do with my hands, my mind, myself, and all the energy I had. I had some noise in my head of all the what ifs, why did I say that, and playing out the future in my head.

This presented some anxiety and social discomfort for me, but when I got sober in 2007, I made a vow that I will enjoy all that life has for me. I went dancing, I hung out with friends, and continued to put myself out there. Through this I began to get that I am enough, and I do not need a substance to enhance my way of being or experience.

I hope you give yourself this divine chance to see all the beauty you hold and were born with. Unfolding all the gifts of a sobriety practice can take time but I promise that the gifts are immeasurable and irreplaceable.

Chapter 9

Meditation Practice

Meditation is becoming more mainstream which makes starting a new practice easier. There are so many resources available to you online with a quick Google and YouTube search. There is probably a center within 20 miles of you to practice. There are so many forms of meditation and ways to meditate that you can't do it wrong.

I started with guided meditation which provides guidance from a teacher during the practice. Meditation to me simply means time spent in introspection, spirit connection, and reflection with integration of mental, emotional, physical, and spiritual experiences. It creates a space for emptying and refilling. Meditation practice attracts more people because of the gifts in peace and calmness it can bring.

I have done various forms of meditation throughout my life and I encourage you to try different methods to find what works for you. Here are some practices you can implement to get you started and motivated:

Start your day with 5 minutes of meditation- then increase it by 5 minutes as you seem ready. You can do this guided, silent, or with music.

Start your day with 15-30 minutes of meditation.

Start your day with a walking meditation- there are some of these guided online.

Start your day with a movement and body connection meditation- pick a few songs and allow your body to move use the breath to guide and loosen your body.

End your day with a Yoga Nidra or a bedtime guided meditation.

End your day with a gratitude meditation- take time to reflect on what you are grateful for.

These practices will definitely be a great fuel to get you jump started.

I have clients that bring their tendency for perfectionism, elitism, and restriction into their practice. It is best to leave these attributes outside of your practice or allow them to unravel in your practice. You are doing it right.

Allow yourself the freedom to know that all meditation practice is great!

Chapter 10

Movement Practice

The way that we take care of our bodies can usually be seen in how we experience life.

If we aren't taking the best care of ourselves, we tend to become overly needy on others, detached, disconnected, and/or find ourselves being abandoned by people- mirroring to us how we have abandoned ourselves.

We must take care of ourselves first and know that we are the only ones responsible for our well-being.

A movement practice is a great tool of support. Such practice will increase energy, shift your physical structure, and enhance both your mental and emotional experience of life. It has been proven that exercise can cause a chemical release of serotonin, endorphins, and dopamine-the "feel good" chemicals.

Movement added into your life regularly can increase your quality of life! Perhaps you already have a movement practice- keep it going!

See what else your body may need in the area of movement. Maybe you're a runner, a crossfitter, or HIIT junkie- your body may need more yoga and mobility or a couple of days of cross-training.

Allow yourself to play with your movement practice, the body likes to change contrary to the mind.

It is best that you commit to a time of day that you can do consistently throughout the week. Early mornings are best for me, it adds energy to my day, gets me pumped, and sets my body up to be an optimal functioning machine. Choose a time, and the timeframe, that you're going to do and commit to it.

If you are new to having a movement practice, have been inconsistent in the past, or have experienced exercise addiction or resistance, try on some of these movement practices:

Go for a walk for 20-30 minutes as soon as you wake up.

Play music and dance for 30 minutes.

Join a gym and choose classes that you'll attend at the same time each day.

Interval train for 30 minutes: walk for 1 minute and run for 30 seconds or run for 1 minute and walk for 30 seconds.

Find a yoga video on YouTube- do it no less than 20 minutes.

Find a dance video on YouTube- do it no less than 20 minutes.

Try a new fitness class.

Life Hack: If you have a schedule that is inconsistent, take time at the beginning of each week to plan when you will commit to your movement practice each day.

*A best practice of self-care is how we nourish our bodies. Choose foods that support you in living in optimal health. As you are harnessing your movement practice, allow it to motivate your nutrition. Allow yourself to eat to fuel, eat for health, and eat for the love of all that you are.

Chapter 11

The Truth

At this point in our journey together you have felt many different sensations on the physical, emotional, mental, and spiritual plane.

Allow any prompts of discomfort or "aha" to guide you deeper into you and your truth. I am here to support you in remembering who you are.

You are a holy entity and a wholly entity.

We were born perfectly and with a specific purpose.

As life happened, we became more and more consumed with lies, distractions we began taking on the truths that society and culture formed for us. This no longer works. We are free to uncover our own truths.

There are endless amounts of resources in the world available to you.

What I want you to remember is simple: you hold the truth within you.

We often get lost in wanting others to tell us our truth or what we should do.

We are the most capable being that we know-we just forget.

You may be queer, you may be a person of color, or a fellow human being. Nothing can keep us back from our light and truth except for ourselves. The universe saw it necessary you to be alive on this day and this lifetime. Take your power back, own your space, and know that you are worthy of the space you occupy.

What is truth for me may not be the truth for you. Give yourself the freedom to explore what your truth is!

Unleash and unbind yourself from the perspective and concepts that have led you to this point. When we wake up to the fact that we have choice and we practice that choice, we are free.

Take time to explore the practices outlined in this book-they will enhance your life.

Thank you for sharing in this journey with me.

Blessings of love and healing to you!

Meet the Author...

I would love to meet you in the real world. I hold workshops, speak, and collaborate all over the world. You can invite me to speak or hold a workshop in your town.

I am here to turn on the light of your soul by igniting your spirit. I facilitate substance-free spiritual ceremonies, ordain weddings and partnership blessing ceremonies.

I offer individual sessions and programing for individual clients creating the perfect culmination of the practices that I have mentioned and much more. I love being able to work with each of you one-on-one.

I'd love to hear from you! I want to know what changes you've been making, of what realizations you're having and what beauty you're creating.

Bliss, Peace, and Wellness,

SW-MM

To view my calendar, schedule a consult or learn more, please visit my website:
www.mysticalminister.com

Made in the USA
Columbia, SC
25 May 2019